I AM HERE!

Living Life to My Fullest Potential ... Celebrating Down Syndrome

Many thanks to the wonderful people who helped create this book:

Teresa Maggit and Shawn Williams

To Kathy Shine for the referral to HenschelHAUS to publish it.

And thank you to Michelle Brewer for her guidance
on our journey to writing this book.

I AM HERE!

Written by Ravaughn Jennings Williams
with Dawn Williams

Henschel HAUS
www.henschelHAUSbooks.com
Milwaukee, Wisconsin

Photographs provided by the author.

Published by
HenschelHAUS Publishing, Inc.
www.henschelHAUSbooks.com
Milwaukee, Wisconsin

ISBN: 979-8-9908203-7-1
LCCN: 2024942737

A portion of the proceeds from the sale of this book go to
GiGi's Playhouse and Friendship Circle.

Printed in the USA.

FOREWORD

I AM HERE is a book about trials and triumphs of being a person with Down Syndrome and raising a person with special needs, all while totally trusting and believing in God. When you read this book, you will see that Down Syndrome is actually a superpower that we all desire and a gift to be envied.

"Von"—Ravaughn Jennings Williams—has a special way of turning your frowns upside down, making bad good, and shows a love and compassion for people that makes everyone feel important and special. His favorite line is, "You are my favorite"—when he says that, he means it and you believe. You will also learn that a lot of the love and compassion he has came from his mother, Dawn, who sees the best in everything. She too has an infectious smile and a gentle but stern way of teaching and reassuring Von.

I am extremely proud and overwhelmed with their life, story, and accomplishments. I'm sure that you will be too.

I love you both and I'm very proud of each of you. I look forward to seeing and learning more from your life experiences.

Love always

"Your Favorite!" Tara

WOW! I AM HERE!

My name is Ravaughn. I was born on the 4th of July
and I came into this world to bring light! I am a
firecracker and I am here to pop and shine!

My mom told me that the day I was born, I had a
head full of soft silky hair and that I was the most
beautiful baby she had ever seen. She said she
looked into my tiny brown eyes and said,
"I love you."

I was born early so I was home for my baby shower. Mom said there were a lot of
family, friends and gifts, but as always I was the highlight of the party.

Although I was small, I had a big heart from the start. It was so big that it must have
exploded inside my mommy's belly because when I was born I had a hole in it and
before I turned 2, I had to have surgery. I was also diagnosed with asthma and Down's
Syndrome. Due to my conditions, the doctors thought I might not live past the age
of 3, but I'm a miracle because *I AM HERE!*

Down Syndrome is a condition that affects how your brain and body develop. It often
causes lack of growth and learning disabilities, but my mom doesn't play when it

Von and Mom

comes to learning and always focuses on my abilities. She always says keep trying, this is how you learn. Mom is my biggest advocate and with the help of family, friends and others I have learned a lot!

To better my development, she keeps me in programs to help me grow. As a baby I attended a program called Birth to Three and it gave me a head start with education and therapies.

Throughout my school years, I had great teachers. Since I graduated, I've been blessed to continue my educational training through programs at Gigi's Playhouse, Friendship Circle, UWM-Milwaukee and more. I'm thankful for them because they have taught me many skills. The best part is I enjoy hanging out with my friends while learning.

They're my favorite!

Here I am exercising with friends at GiGi's Playhouse

Friendship Circle

GiGi's Playhouse

Fun Fact: World Down Syndrome Day is celebrated March 21 every year.

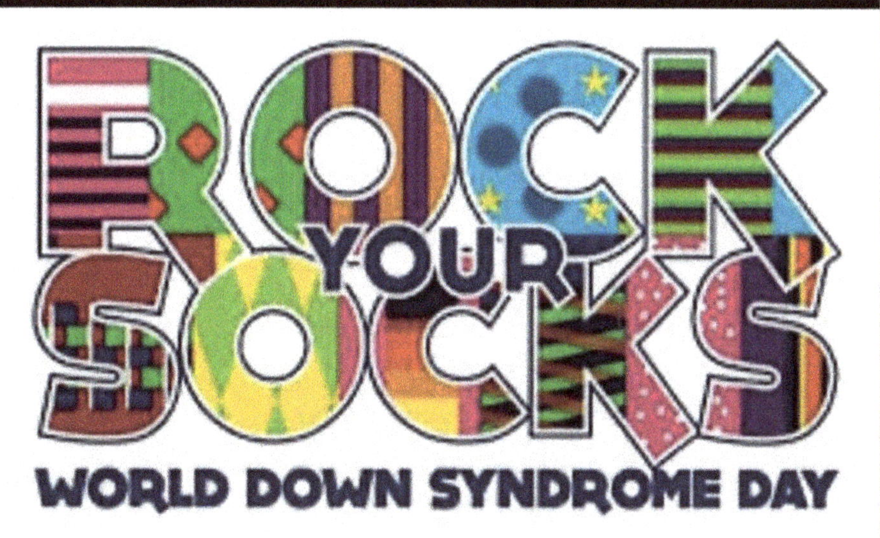

On World Down Syndrome Day, we rock and mix and match socks too!

God has been a big part of my life. I grew up in the church and we dressed up a lot. My mom sometimes tells me stories about when I was much smaller and younger. My great-grandma was always there for me. She took me to church and many other places. We had a big church and I still remember how much fun we had.

Once, Granny took me with other church members to Georgia on an airplane. I was scared. I didn't like flying then and I don't like it now! But I'm still a firecracker... I just prefer to be a bang on the ground.

Calvary Intl. Worship Center (formally Mt. Cavalry Holy Church of America)

At church, they serve food, and my favorites would feed me. I remember that, because I love food! They would feed me stuff like chicken and beer. Well, it was root beer of course, but I just liked to say beer because I would get a laugh every time. I would ask for it every Sunday and watch them crack up laughing. This is still funny; can you imagine being at church and asking for beer? Yup, that was me! This is when my mom first realized that I was a comedian, and my audience was the church. I would pray for people and much more. Church people are my favorite. So is my great-grandma.

Here I'm with my Great-grandma

She bought me nice suits when I was little because I said I wanted to be a preacher. Can you imagine me being a preacher? I would be a funny preacher because I make people laugh.

I still go to church, dress nicely, and make people laugh. That hasn't changed. That's why I'm here—to lift people's spirits!

My family always looked out for me—and they still do. People underestimate my abilities.

Did you know I had my very own business before? I sold my very own oil sprays.

Me and my mom

I can do a lot of things, even if I sometimes need help.

I tell my family I can do stuff, but they still try to do things for me anyway. Usually I just let them help, unless my mom is around. She butts in and tells me to do it myself. Sometimes I like when people help me.

Not only am I spoiled,
but I'm an uncle and
my nieces are spoiled
just like me. I get to
help and teach them. I
love them—they are
my favorites.

Daijah, one of my sisters.
She is my favorite!

I have two sisters and one brother.

My sister Daijah is six years younger than me. When we were little, she would always help me. My mom would say, "Stop helping him. He can do it." Daijah would sneak and help me anyway.

My sister Tiffany and brother CJ
They are my favorite, too!

Cooking at GiGi's Playhouse

Cooking with Uncle Vic

That's why I'm here—to let people help me. It makes them feel good to do nice things for me. I'm spoiled!

Cooking with Diane
at GiGi's Playhouse

At school, the kids would always tie my shoes. That was until the teacher mentioned that to my mom. My mom busted me out and told the teacher that I knew how to tie my shoes myself.

I am 33 years old now in 2024. I am a grown man and I try to be independent. I have my own man cave. I can do many

things. I can't do everything—like drive—but I am still growing and will continue learning as long as I AM HERE!

I also enjoy sports and parties. I play basketball with the Special Olympics Team. I go to professional wrestling matches and bas-

ketball games. I go to sports parties and wear my sports gear and eat good food! The Bucks, Cowboys, Packers, and Brewers are my favorite teams, at least when they are winning.

Glow party!!! What fun!!

Every year, MY birthday is always a blast! I have a whole bunch of food and a hip DJ with lots of family and friends. They know how to turn up, but of course, I am the life of the party. Just like Chris Brown, I am a dancing machine. I'm always the last one on the floor.

Celebrating with family and friends

End of the night Birthday Bash with family, friends, and Clark Kent (green shirt) who has been my personal DJ since I was 18.

Getting my dance moves ready before the party starts.

Another year with friends, family, and my personal DJ,

Clark Kent.

Showing out at a family gathering.

Did you know that I am also famous? Well, at least in my eyes.

I was born to be a star.

I've even been on television as a spokesperson for Gigi's a few times. At Friendship Circle, I was interviewed by the news. I have a manager, chauffeurs, bodyguards and a big fan club!

My family and friends are some of my biggest fans.

I love my fans, especially the ladies! The ladies love me! *They are my favorite!*

I've even met famous people like me. I won't mention all of them but here are a few.

I've attended gospel concerts and met gospel recording artist Tasha Cobbs.

Attending the play, "When a Woman's Fed Up" starring Patrice Lovely aka Hattie Mae.

Me and former Milwaukee Bucks player John Henson at GiGi's Playhouse.

My mom is my biggest fan. She is also my manager. She believes in me, and she is tough! She always looks out for me. She buys me nice things like clothes and shoes to look nice because you never know when the paparazzi are watching. She takes me places like out-of-town and out to eat. I love to eat, but because I have health problems, she makes sure I don't overdo it. I know she loves me and only wants what's best for me.

Me and my mom

My dad is pretty cool. He is in Tennessee now and I go and visit him sometimes. I'm glad we drive there instead of flying. We have a family reunion almost every year. I love to visit my family—they are my favorite. They love to cook, and I love to eat! We always have fun, and I am the life of the party. I love music and I love to dance so I get the party poppin', just like I do on my birthday!

Me and my dad

Then there's my tete Shawn (my mother's sister). She is the best tete ever! She really is my favorite. She takes me places and plays video games with me and makes me laugh really hard. When we are in the car, she sings, and I tell her don't quit your day job. She loves me and she's a big fan! She even created a Facebook page for me. Her followers are my fans too! On her Facebook page, I get so many likes.

I have a lot of other fans as well...but I would never finish this book if I were to list them all. I love them and they are all my favorite.

Me and my Aunt Shawn

Me and my Aunt Shawn

"You're My Favorite" is my famous quote. I always call people who are nice to me *"my favorite,"* because it makes them smile and I like to make people happy. **That is why I AM HERE!**

I'm glad I made it into the world! I'm blessed to be here. I have a good life, loving family and a wonderful support system. Life hasn't always been perfect or easy, but I am here!

Me and Auntie Shaunda

Me and Uncle Vic

MY FAMILY AND FRIENDS SUPPORT SYSTEM

I show through my life that even in the things that seem helpless and small,
there is hope.

I live to create a spark.

I enjoy my life and you should too.

I am here because God has a plan for me.

I am here to help people.

I am here to make people feel special.

I am here to make people happy.

I am here to show love.

I am here because I am a miracle.

I am here to show everyone I can learn without limitations.

I am here to show everyone that I am smart.

I am here because I am supposed to be here.

I am here to live.

I am here to laugh.

I am here to love.

My name is to be remembered. Ravaughn is my name, and I AM HERE!

Contact information:
Email: Vonlibrary@gmail.com
Facebook: AuthorRavaughnWilliams